ECHO
CHAMBERS

INSIDE AMERICA'S POLITICAL DIVIDE

Joanne Carter, M.Ed.

Paperback: 978-1-963883-61-9
Hardback: 978-1-963883-82-4
eBook: 978-1-963883-62-6
Library of Congress Control Number: 2024906402

Ordering Information:

Prime Seven Media
518 Landmann St.
Tomah City, WI 54660

Printed in the United States of America

Disclaimer:

This document's information is for educational and entertainment purposes only. All efforts have been made to provide accurate, up-to-date, dependable, and complete information. Warranties of any kind are declared or implied. Readers acknowledge that the author is not engaged in legal, medical, financial, or professional advice. Consult a licensed professional before attempting techniques or acting on the information outlined in this book.

By reading this document, the reader agrees that under no circumstance is the author responsible for any direct or indirect losses incurred because of the use of the information within this document. This includes, but is not limited to, errors, omissions, or inaccuracies.

Table of Contents

Introduction

Echo chambers are enclosed spaces where sound reverberates. It is also an environment where a person meets only people who believe or have opinions that agree with their existing views. These are reinforced, and alternatives are not considered. We, the people, are living in partisan ideological echo chambers.

Forces of religion, society, and culture have collided in a three-car collision at a four-stop intersection. The fourth car is still driving; with an upcoming election, the result may be another January 6th even if Joe Biden has a landslide victory, a logical consequence based on what we have already seen. Republicans have been planning Project 2025.

White evangelists famously were responsible for 81% of the 2016 votes. It is easy to fear the possibility that we may have to endure another crisis if this election is close. As the results are contested, then recounted, perhaps invalidated by one party. We may have a president for whom we did not vote.

I would say that these things are known:

1. We tend to cluster in like-minded communities.

2. We become more fervent When surrounded by people who agree with us.

3. Approximately 80% of Americans live under the rule of one party. (Trifecta states)

4. We can feel the tension of the "Cold Civil War" in the air. Many commentators have called it such.

5. The speaker of the House is a fervent believer, self-described. He is second in line for the presidency behind Kamala Harris.

6. There is a project 2025 Republicans have been working on for the past two years. What does that imply?

In the past four years, I have heard and read about fervent partisans, including members of the current Congress, who describe and theorize on television about a second Civil War. Some of these characters aim to create civil conflict and bitter bickering with outrageous and theatrical performances.

We must start to think beyond our tribe and deliberately care for the state of our nation. As world citizens, we must get beyond the name-calling and the daily clown acts the media shows us on television and social media. We see protestors and worldwide news. Globally, politics are in crisis in Ukraine, Gaza, Russia, Israel, China, North Korea, and Taiwan. There may be an authoritarian movement globally. The globalization of media content allows for the dissemination of diverse viewpoints and comparing domestic policies and politics with those of other countries, broadening the scope of political discourse and potentially influencing opinions on domestic policies. The media's impact on shaping political opinions operates through various mechanisms that affect the content of political discourse and how the public processes and understands political information.

The media's traditional role as a watchdog holding public officials and institutions accountable is crucial in shaping political opinions by uncovering misconduct, corruption, or policy failures.

It is essential in shaping political views by exposing misconduct, corruption, or policy failures. Investigative journalism can lead to significant public and political reactions and considerable public responses.

The two major political parties in the United States, the Democratic and Republican parties, correspond closely with liberal and conservative ideologies. These ideologies influence US policy debates, often concerning the appropriate government intervention in the economy and social behavior.

There is a strong correlation between individuals' Ideology and their party choice; Americans hold various opinions on economic and social issues. They do not fit neatly into a left or a right column.

Conduct a respectful, even curious conversation with someone across the divide without being disdainful so the other person does not feel threatened or bullied.

CHAPTER 1

The Roots of Division

The roots of America's political divide can be traced back to the country's founding. The federalists and anti-federalists debated over the size and power of the federal government.

The dominant political parties and ideologies are:

Conservative Ideology: Conservatives believe the government should be small, operating at the state or local level. Social conservatives believe that the government should uphold traditional morality. Conservatives are said to fall on the right wing of the axis of political beliefs.

Democratic Party: One of the two main political parties in the United States, founded in 1828 by supporters of Andrew Jackson. The Democratic Party is the world's oldest active political party. Today, the core values of the Democratic Party align with liberal Ideology.

Liberal Ideology: the definition of liberalism has changed over time, but modern-day liberals tend to believe that government should intervene in the economy and provide a broad range of social services to ensure well-being and equality across society. They do not think that the government should regulate private sexual or social behaviors.

Progressive Ideology: Progressive is used interchangeably at times with liberal by people. Those who consider these terms separate Say that liberals believe in protecting previously disadvantaged groups from discrimination. In contrast, progressives think it is the government's job to address past wrongs and reform systemic issues that cause these disadvantages in the first place.

The Green Party: this is the fourth largest party on the register. It stands for primarily pro-environmental causes.

Democratic Party

(The Super cheesy pizza)

Big Ideas: they think the government should help people, especially those who need extra support, like people who do not have much money or are sick.

On Helping People: they want to ensure everyone has access to good doctors and schools and believe in making rules to protect the environment.

On Money: they think the government should spend money to make these things happen, even if it means higher taxes, especially for wealthy people.

Republican Party

(The crunchy salad)

Big Ideas: they believe people should have more freedom to make their own choices without the government being too involved.

On Helping People: They think the best way to help people is by letting businesses grow without too many rules, which they believe will create more jobs and opportunities.

On Money: they prefer lower taxes for everyone, including businesses, believing that this hope helps the economy grow and gives people more freedom to spend their money how they want.

It could be like choosing between pizza and salad; people in the U.S. often lean towards one party or the other based on which recipe they think is best for the country. It is also okay to like some ideas from both and sometimes to launch changes in options, and then parties can change.

Republicans tend to favor conservative policies, too. We must figure out how to run the country best. I would not say a dictatorship would allow us to have any say.

However, if the election turns out, there will be repercussions, quite serious, difficulties to follow.

We must choose between Autocracy and Democracy this time.

Both candidates are self-described.

Republicans tend to favor conservative policies, emphasizing limited government, free marketplace principles, individual liberties, and traditional values.

Cultural values and regional identities play a significant role in the divide. Urban areas tend to lean towards more liberal ideas. Rural areas are often more conservative. These differences are political and deeply rooted in their way of life, economic interests, and social values. The blood will divide in the USA. It is deeply entrenched and affects every part of American life. Comprehending this divide requires an appreciation of the country's history, culture, and the diverse perspectives of its citizens.

The structure of the U.S. electoral system, including the Electoral College, gerrymandering, and voting restrictions, can exaggerate political divisions. These mechanisms sometimes result in disproportionate representation and intensify feelings of disenfranchisement among voters.

Central to the democratic party's beliefs is that the economy should work for everyone, not just the wealthy or privileged. The Democrats advocate for health care as a fundamental right for all citizens, emphasizing the importance of affordable, quality health care. The party also reflects diversity as a strength of the nation and is committed to defending and promoting democratic values and practices. Its platform addresses various issues, from economic policy supporting working families and the middle class to Environmental Protection and educational reform.

The rise of political polarization in the United States in recent decades has been marked by an increasing ideological division between the two major political parties and among the electorate. This polarization is evident in the stances on specific issues and the general approach to governance and political discourse. Several factors have contributed to this phenomenon.

Democrats tend to support government intervention to address economic inequality and discrimination.

Republicans favor a free market approach with minimal government interference.

Republican-leaning groups include the Faith Conservatives, The Conservatives, The populist Right, and the Maga Cult.

Republican Faith Conservatives are intensely conservative in all ways. Many believe that government policies should reflect religious values and that negotiation in politics is selling out what you believe in.

Conservatives also have traditional values but are not obsessed with bringing religious beliefs into legislation. They seem less intense but tend to vote party line and favor businesses, corporations, and tax cuts for the wealthy. They call Social Security and Medicare "entitlement" programs, which they propose eliminating yearly.

The Populist Right Republicans usually have less formal education, are among the most likely to live in rural areas, and are critical of immigration policies and US Corporations.

(https://www.pewresearch.com)

At the heart of these divisions are fundamental disagreements on critical issues such as economic policy, social welfare, health care, environmental regulation, gun control, abortion, and immigration. Democrats advocate for more stringent environmental rules and a more significant role of the government in providing social services and more excellent protection for civil rights.

Our efforts to bridge the political divide in the United States might involve initiatives to foster dialogue, promote media literacy, and encourage political systems and processes that prioritize collaboration over partisanship. We also seek to create a more inclusive and understanding political environment. We cannot allow political disagreements to lead to social ostracization and harassment or give rise to extremist groups and actions.

Ukraine depends on the United States' aid to keep fighting. Congress inaction has curtailed the flow of supplies, and Ukrainian units must erase their ammunition, conceding to the artillery advantage that the Russians have. Israel has mobilized so many troops to fight Hamas that its civilian economy is diminished. Twelve hundred Israelis were either taken hostage or were slaughtered and raped. Israel has massacred over 25,000 Palestinian civilians, half of whom were children.

Republicans insist on linking Ukraine and Israel to border enforcement. They have refused to bring this bill to the floor. This is reportedly because candidate Trump does not want Biden awarded any win, especially if it involves border security. He wants to use it as an election issue.

Congress can and should reform the still much-abused asylum system, and really, it should rewrite the law. We need more judges to process the new mass of claims. The faster the claims are heard, the sooner the rejected applicants can be removed. Joe Biden has made this part of his legislation, which the Republicans refuse to vote on.

Media Landscape Changes:

Fragmentation: the advent of cable news and the Internet has led to a fragmented media landscape, where news outlets often cater to specific audiences. This has resulted in echo chambers, where individuals are primarily exposed to information and viewpoints reinforcing their preexisting beliefs.

Social media: Platforms like Facebook, Twitter, Instagram, Discord, and YouTube have transformed how information is disseminated and consumed, amplifying polarization by enabling the rapid spread of misinformation and partisan content.

Social media raises concern over the accuracy of the information. They do allow for instantaneous communication. A cell phone is a fantastic tool, but it can be misused to form and strengthen echo chambers while providing a dopamine surge.

Political Realignment: the parties have become more ideologically homogeneous over the past few years. The Democrats have moved further to the left, while the Republicans have shifted to the right.

Cultural and Demographic Shifts: Changes in the demographic composition of the United States, including increased racial and ethnic diversity, changing religions, and evolving social norms, have contributed to political polarization. Diverse groups have distinct political priorities and values, which are increasingly aligned with one party or the other. Cultural issues, such as gun rights, abortion, and LGBTQ plus rights, have become more central to party identities, worsening divisions.

Electoral and Political System Factors: gerrymandering, the practice of drawing electoral district boundaries to benefit one party, has intensified polarization by creating safe seats for both parties, reducing the incentive for politicians to appeal to the political center. Primary elections often reward candidates who appeal to the most ideologically committed voters, pushing other officials further to the ideological extremes.

This has intensified polarization by creating safe seats for both parties and reducing the incentive for politicians to appeal to the political center.

Economic inequality: Growing economic disparities and perceptions of economic injustice have fueled political divisions, with different parties proposing vastly different solutions. This has made monetary policy a more polarizing subject.

Psychological and Social Dynamics: group identity and tribalism have become a more pronounced part of politics, with party affiliation becoming a significant part of an individual's identity. This us versus them mentality exacerbates conflicts and reduces the willingness to compromise.

The Role of Political Leadership: Political figures have increasingly employed divisive rhetoric, framing political competition as a battle between good and evil, further entrenching divisions. Leadership styles that embrace confrontation over consensus have contributed to polarization. They are a RED Flag!

Consequences of Polarization: the rise in polarization has had profound implications for American governance and society, including:

Legislative Gridlock: increased difficulty in passing legislation and managing the government as a compromise becomes politically risky.

Social Fragmentation: Deepening social divides, with polarization affecting not just political views but also choices about where to live, whom to associate with, and consumer behavior.

Violating Democratic Norms increases skepticism about the legitimacy of political opponents and institutions, leading to challenges in democratic governance and civil discourse.

The Political Divide is a complex and multifaceted issue with no single cause or easy solution. It reflects deep-seated changes in society, technology, and the political landscape, requiring concerted efforts across multiple fronts to address.

Listening, being honest, even curious, and having face-to-face, civil, and respectful conversations with those in opposition can help both sides learn something.

The scope of a book that covers the political divide in the United States and its implications on elections requires focusing on key themes and issues.

A general overview of potential dangers and challenges that could be associated with the presidential election include:

Disinformation and Misinformation: the spread of false or misleading information, primarily through social media, can manipulate public opinion, sow discord, and undermine the integrity of the electoral process.

Foreign Interference: Concerns about foreign entities attempting to interfere in the election through cyberattacks, disinformation campaigns, or other means potentially threatening the democratic process, such as receiving monetary incentives, loans, or gifts from adversarial nations.

Election Security: ensuring the security of voting systems and preventing hacking or tampering is crucial. Any vulnerabilities in the election infrastructure could undermine the legitimacy of its results. Donald Trump and Rudy Guiliani created many bizarre lies to stay in power!

Voter Suppression: efforts to suppress voter turnout through restrictive voting laws, gerrymandering, or other tactics can undermine the democratic principle of free and fair elections. There are gerrymandered seats (safe seats) for each side!

Polarization and Divisiveness: a highly polarized political environment can contribute to social tensions and create a climate of hostility. This may lead to protests, civil unrest, and even violence.

Election Challenges: disputes over the election results, recounts, or legal difficulties can create uncertainty and erode public confidence. A contested election leads to prolonged uncertainty.

Some factions of the present Republican Party have refused to concede the loss of an election—the peaceful transfer of power.

The political divide in the United States is characterized by profound ideological and partisan differences between the two major political parties. Several key issues contribute to this division:

Policy Differences: Democrats and Republicans often have divergent views on health care, immigration, gun control, climate change, and economic policies. These policy differences reflect broader ideological distinctions.

Cultural and Social Issues: The parties also differ on cultural and social issues, including abortion, LGBTQ+ rights, and racial justice. These differences contribute to polarization and shape voters' party affiliations.

Media influence: Media outlets with different political orientations can contribute to the divide by presenting news and information in ways that align with their respective ideologies. The Media also creates echo chambers where individuals are exposed to information reinforcing their beliefs.

Geographical Split: there is often a geographical split, with urban areas leaning Democratic and the rural regions leaning Republican. The urban-rural divide can amplify political differences.

Polarization in Congress: the polarization extends to the legislative branch, where members of Congress often vote along party lines. This can lead to legislative gridlock and a lack of bipartisan cooperation. A congress that accomplishes almost nothing.

Populist Movements on both the left and right have gained prominence, expressing dissatisfaction with the political establishment and contributing to a sense of discontent and division.

Identity Politics: identity politics, based on race, gender, and ethnicity, play a significant role in shaping political opinions and alliances. This can further polarize the electorate.

Elections and Campaigns: Political campaigns and elections can contribute to polarization, with candidates often adopting more extreme positions to appeal to their party's base during primary elections. The political landscape is dynamic, and the issues contributing to the divide may evolve. **Public opinion, leadership styles, and external events also shape the political climate.**

The political divide in the United States has deep historical roots. Understanding these factors provides insight into the current state of American politics.

Founding Ideas vs. Practical Governance: from the nation's inception, there was a divide between the Federalists, who advocated for a strong central government, and the Anti-federalists, who feared centralized power and preferred more authority for the states. This early division laid the groundwork for future political divides.

Civil War Reconstruction: The Civil War was pivotal, with the divide primarily over slavery and states' rights. Post-war reconstruction further deepened divisions, particularly between the North and South, over how to reintegrate southern states and how to treat freed slaves.

The Progressive Era: In the late 19th and early 20th centuries, the progressive movement sought to address problems caused by industrialization and urbanization, leading to a divide between those pushing for reform and those resisting it to preserve the status quo.

New Deal Politics: Franklin D Roosevelt's New Deal created a new alignment, with Democrats becoming the party of expansive government intervention in the economy, which was opposed by Republicans who favored less government involvement.

Civil Rights Movement: the 1960s civil rights movement further realigned political parties, with the Democrats increasingly supporting civil rights, leading to a shift where many were opposed by Republicans who favored less government involvement.

(https://www.fbmarketplace.org/)

CHAPTER 2

The Partisan Divide

Cultural and Regional Differences

Urban vs. Rural: Urban areas tend to be democratic, valuing diversity and progressive social policies, while rural areas often support Republican values like individualism and traditional social norms.

Coastal vs. Heartland: Coastal areas, both on the Pacific and Atlantic, are more often liberal, Whereas Heartland and the South tend to be more conservative, reflecting different economic interests, lifestyles, and cultural values.

Both parties have internal divisions. Among Democrats, there is a split between progressives, who pushed for more radical reforms like universal healthcare and aggressively addressing climate change, and moderates, who advocated for incremental change.

Among Republicans, we have the Maga faction and the conservatives who vote along party lines.

Republicans have divisions between establishment conservatives, who focus on fiscal conservatism and international engagement, and more populist or nationalist factions, prioritizing issues like immigration control and skepticism towards global institutions. Issues like gun rights, religion in public life, and attitudes toward immigration and abortion also reflect a deep cultural divide.

Republicans have traditionally pursued lower taxes, especially for companies and wealthy individuals with higher taxpayer burdens. They are often for less federal regulation of the environment and the economy. As a result of this anti-regulation stance, republicans are typically proponents of certain individual rights, notably gun ownership. The party opposes affirmative action and organized labor. It has a long-standing goal of trimming or eliminating government-funded social programs like Social Security and Medicare to reduce government spending. The GOP is more comfortable regulating the private non-economic sphere, backing hard limits on abortion and LGBTQ Plus+ rights, and often works to insert Judea-Christian prayer into public life.

Democrats advocate for more progressive policies, including a more significant role for the government in providing social services, more stringent environmental regulations, and greater protections for civil rights. At the heart of this divide are fundamental disagreements such as economic policy, social welfare, health care, environmental regulations, gun control, abortion, and immigration.

The role of the media may have been transformative in shaping and reinforcing the political divide. Social media platforms amplify and create echo chambers, where users are exposed primarily to the viewpoints they already have, further entrenching divisions.

The political divide has significant implications for governance, leading to legislative gridlock, hyperpartisanship, and challenges in addressing critical national issues. It has permeated everyday life, affecting social interactions, community cohesion, and even familial relationships, with increasing instances of political extremism and violence. This has contributed to an environment where political disagreements can lead to social ostracization, harassment, or worse, give rise to extreme groups and actions of violence.

The civil harassment suits of Rudy Guiliani and Donald Trump demonstrate these actions and behaviors.

The typical political landscape consists of many divisions within each of the parties.

The Democratic-leaning groups are the Progressive Left, the Establishment Left, and The Democratic Loyalists.

The Progressive Left is the only majority-white, non-Hispanic group who have very liberal ideas on every issue. They attempt to correct racial, social, and environmental injustices and expand the social safety nets. They believe that situations that have been fundamentally biased need to be rebuilt systemically.

The Establishment Liberals, while as liberal as the Progressives, are not easily persuaded of the necessity for sweeping change. **The Loyalists** will vote for the party. They are usually the oldest and unwavering. Their projected general attitude appears that these changes must occur but can be reworked within the system.

Republican-leaning groups include the Faith Conservatives, The Conservatives, The populist Right, and the Maga Cult.

Republican Faith Conservatives are intensely conservative in all ways. Many believe that government policies should reflect religious values and that negotiation in politics is selling out what you believe in.

Conservatives also have traditional values but are not obsessed with bringing religious beliefs into legislation. They seem less intense but tend to vote party line and favor businesses, corporations, and tax cuts for the wealthy. They call Social Security and Medicare "entitlement" programs, which they propose eliminating yearly.

The Populist Right Republicans usually have less formal education, are among the most likely to live in rural areas, and are critical of immigration policies and US Corporations.

(https://www.pewresearch.com)

Republican Party: One of the two main political parties in the United States. They were founded in 1854 by anti-slavery activists. The party has transformed over the years to address the issues of concern with its constituents, which aligns with conservative Ideology.

The Republican Party aims to preserve American values and traditions and restore the American dream for every citizen. They support policies that stimulate economic growth, protect constitutionally guaranteed freedoms, and ensure election integrity. They emphasize reducing taxes for the wealthy, advocating states' rights, and supporting National Defense. They tend to oppose extensive government regulation and government-funded social programs.

CHAPTER 3

The Media and the Divide

The media landscape has a significant impact on the political divide. Traditional media outlets often have perceived biases that cater to specific political leanings, reinforcing preexisting beliefs. The rise of social media and digital news has further amplified this divide, creating echo chambers where individuals are exposed primarily to viewpoints that align with their own, reducing exposure to opposing perspectives.

The political divide has real-world implications for social cohesion, community relations, and personal relationships. It has contributed to an environment where political disagreements can lead to social ostracization, harassment, or, even worse, giving rise to extremist groups and actions. Efforts to bridge the political divide involve fostering dialogue, promoting media literacy, and encouraging political systems and processes prioritizing collaboration over partisanship. This divide affects every aspect of

American life. To seek a more inclusive and understanding appreciation for diverse perspectives is needed.

The media plays a crucial role in shaping political opinions, serving as the primary conduit through which most people receive information about politics, policies, and public affairs. Several aspects illustrate the media's role in shaping political opinions. The press chooses which stories to highlight and how frequently to carry them to cover them. This shapes the public agenda, making specific issues more important. They also frame those issues in particular ways, influencing the perception and interpretation of the audience. Media coverage can prime viewers to use specific criteria to evaluate political figures or policies. Extensive coverage of an issue may lead people to prioritize a particular candidate's policies more. The media's traditional role as a watchdog that holds public officials and institutions accountable is crucial. The media's impact on shaping political opinions is profound, operating through various mechanisms that influence the content of political discourse and how the public processes and understands political information.

Social Media

Social media and digital platforms have changed how information is shared and assumed, significantly impacting public discussions and amplifying societal divisions. These vital mechanisms can explain their role in exacerbating political and social divisions.

Echo Chambers: Social media platforms tend to create echo chambers, where users are exposed to information and opinions reinforcing their beliefs and biases.

Algorithms that curate content based on past user engagement contribute to this effect, limiting exposure to diverse perspectives and entrenching users further in their viewpoints.

Selective exposure: Users often select sources and communities that align with their beliefs, leading to selective exposure. This self-selection into white ideologically homogeneous groups reduces the chance of encountering challenging or moderating viewpoints, contributing to polarization.

The breaking speed of misinformation: social media facilitates the fast and widespread dissemination of misinformation and disinformation. False information can go viral quickly, especially if it is sensational or lines with prevalent biases, further entrenching false beliefs and contributing to division.

Anonymity: A lack of face-to-face interaction provides relative anonymity. Digital platforms can encourage users to express extreme views without fearing social or personal repercussions.

CHAPTER 4

Election Mechanics and the Divide

Political campaigns and elections contribute to political division, with candidates often adopting more extreme positions to appeal to their party's base during primary elections. Populist movements on both sides have gained prominence, expressing dissatisfaction with the political situation and contributing to discontent and division.

This polarization extends to the legislative branch; we have members of Congress who vote along party lines. This can lead to legislative gridlock and a lack of bipartisan cooperation. Identity politics based on factors such as race, gender, and ethnicity also can divide the electorate. It plays a significant role in shaping political opinions and alliances, further polarizing the electorate.

In 2016, Donald Trump won the electoral college votes.

However, he did not win the popular vote. **The Electoral College System** allows approximately seventeen states out of fifty to decide the presidential election results. Efforts to suppress voter turnout can undermine the democratic principle of free and fair elections. Populist movements play a significant role in shaping opinions and alliances. Political orientations align with their respective ideologies, further entrenching the divide.

The Electoral College system does not necessarily represent all the voters.

In a national, random sampling survey of over 5000 US adults in 2022, only 28% of the public was satisfied with the performance of Congress. The favorable ratings of Congress continue to decline. Democrats are twice as likely (36% vs.18%) to have a favorable view of Congress.

(www.pewresearch.org).

The public faults both parties for having few promising ideas. Only 41%-44% of either party claimed their parties had innovative ideas, while 27% saw few promising ideas from either party.

Both parties agree that family, friends, and careers add meaning to their lives. They differ, however, on other factors such as health and faith. Only nine percent of Republicans mention health, whereas 13% of Democrats mentioned health and well-being. However, about 22% of Republicans are likely to mention faith and religion as a significantly important part of their lives; among Evangelicals, the percentage is as high as 34%. This is a heavily Republican subgroup.

Partisanship is more connected to the meaning of life in America than in other areas. Factors that add meaning to life differ significantly only in spirituality, faith, and religion for Republicans. It is 14% higher in importance in Republicans, and no other factors, including freedom and independence, hobbies and recreation, and physical and mental health. These factors are a source of meaning in life; otherwise, they are not dramatically different in either party. The Supporters of a party are more likely to mention it as a source of meaning. Within the general undescribed population, it is only 10%.

It is consistent with many Republican party efforts to establish Christian-Judeo Norms as the legislature. I have always believed that in this country, state and religion were to remain separate.

(Pew Research Center, 2024)

Feedback loops: Social media platforms often create feedback loops through likes, shares, and comments, which can validate and reinforce divisive content. Content that generates solid emotional reactions is more likely to be engaged with, creating an incentive to produce more extreme or sensational content.

Fragmentation and Niche Platforms: The best landscape of digital platforms allows for the formation of highly specialized communities. While this can foster a sense of belonging among like-minded individuals, it can also lead to the fragmentation of public discourse into isolated niches, reducing consensus-building opportunities.

Algorithmic bias: Algorithms are designed to maximize engagement, but they can inadvertently amplify divisive content by prioritizing material that provokes strong reactions. This can skew users' perceptions of public opinion and the importance of specific issues, leading to a distorted view of societal divisions.

Groups: Online discussions within homogeneous groups can lead to group polarization, where members' views become more extreme after discussing them with the group. This phenomenon is exacerbated on social media and digital platforms due to the ease of forming and joining such groups.

Harassment and Trolling: The relative ease of targeting individuals on social media platforms can lead to harassment and trolling, especially against those expressing minority or unpopular opinions. This can discourage open and honest communication, further deepening divisions as individuals retreat to safer, more homogeneous online spaces.

Globalization of Divisions: social media and digital platforms extend national boundaries, allowing for the globalization of divisions. Ideological conflicts and polarizing content from one country can influence perceptions and politics in another, spreading division beyond its original context.

In summary, social media and digital platforms play a complex role in amplifying societal divisions. They can reinforce echo chambers, spread misinformation rapidly, and encourage polarization through their inherent structures and algorithms. Addressing these challenges requires a multi-pronged approach, including platform governance, media literacy education, and fostering online environments that encourage exposure to different perspectives.

CHAPTER 5

Flashpoints of Division

Specific issues have become flashpoints in the political divide, including but not limited **to abortion, gun rights, immigration, education, health care, Social Security, Medicare, and climate change**. These issues are highly polarizing and serve as rallying points for political and social mobilization.

There are fundamental disagreements on critical issues such as economic policy, social welfare, health care, environmental regulation, gun control, abortion, and immigration. Democrats advocate for more progressive policies, including a more significant role for the government in providing social services, more stringent environmental regulations, and greater protections for civil rights. Republicans tend to favor conservative policies, emphasizing limited government, pre-marketing principles, individual liberties, and traditional values. Over time, various issues, including states' rights, slavery, and civil rights, have further divided, shaping the modern political landscape.

Roe v.s. Wade: the Supreme Court has overturned Roe vs Wade; local boards of education are banning books due to issues related to race, gender, and sexual orientation. We are closing off readers to people, places, and perspectives. **Religions in the United States have begun attacking books for disagreeing with their religious beliefs.**

The states that have banned books in 2022 include Texas (438), Florida (367), Missouri (315), Utah (109), South Carolina (109), Pennsylvania, North Dakota, Michigan, Colorado, Oklahoma, Wyoming, Missouri, Virginia, North Carolina, New Hampshire, Tennessee, Arkansas, New York, Rhode Island. There have been 1447 total book bans and 874 unique titles.

There have been many incidents since Roe was overturned of states prosecuting women after they have a miscarriage. Many women have needed to be close to death with sepsis due to this conservatism, bought and paid for with dark money, lavish vacations, and other unreported payoffs to at least two Supreme Court Justices.

There have been quite a few new stories of women who have gone into sepsis and are close to death. The Governor of Texas, Greg Abbott, overruled a state court that granted permission to a woman for an abortion due to her life-threatening condition. She had to leave the state and now, due to the damage to her fallopian tubes, may not be able to conceive.

She could investigate in-vitro fertilization. The new "Pro-life" movement focuses on claiming that the frozen egg is a human being.

States are not allowing parents to move their eggs out of the state.

1. How can a human being be property of the state before they are alive?

There is another state that will not allow you to leave if you are pregnant and claims it will prosecute any person who assists you.

CHAPTER 6

The Human Cost

The political divide in the USA has significant human costs impacting various aspects of life and society.

Mental Health Deterioration: The intense political polarization can lead to increased stress, anxiety, and even depression among people who find themselves caught in the crossfire of divisive rhetoric and contentious politics. This can be especially pronounced during election cycles when hot-button issues dominate the news cycle. The constant barrage of political conflict in media and online platforms can deepen feelings of hopelessness and division, leading to a decline in mental well-being.

Erosion of social cohesion: Political divides constrain personal relationships, leading to broken friendships, family ties, and community bonds. When political affiliations become central to one's identity, it can create an us versus them mentality. This can result in social isolation, reduced community engagement, and a lack of trust in cooperation that is essential for addressing common societal challenges.

Impact on public health and health care: political polarization can hinder effective public health responses, especially during the covid 19 pandemic. Differing political views, such as mask mandates, vaccines, and lockdown measures, have led to inconsistent adherence to public health guidelines, contributing to preventable illness, death, and extended strain on healthcare systems. Politicizing healthcare health measures can also lead to underfunded public health initiatives and disparities in healthcare access and outcomes.

Political divisions have undermined effective public health responses to crises, most notably observed during the COVID-19 pandemic. Divergent political views on measures such as mask mandates, social distancing, and vaccinations have led to inconsistent adherence to public health guidelines, contributing to higher rates of infection, hospitalization, and death. The politicization of health measures not only impacts those directly affected by the virus but also strains healthcare systems, healthcare workers, and the overall well-being of communities.

Obstruction of Effective Governance and Policymaking: The political divide often leads to legislative gridlock, which is the inability of lawmakers to reach across the aisle, resulting in stalled legislation, including bills that address critical issues such as poverty, education, and infrastructure. This can have direct human costs, such as inadequate social services, deteriorating infrastructure, and underfunded education systems, disproportionately affecting vulnerable populations.

Increase in Violence and Civil Unrest: Heightened political tensions can lead to a rise in civil unrest, violent protests, and, in extreme cases, acts of terrorism. Political divisiveness, on the other hand, can encourage radical groups and individuals, leading to violent confrontations and attacks. This not only results in physical form and loss of life but also contributes to a climate of fear and division, further entrenching political divides.

The human toll highlights the pervasive effect of political polarization. The division affects the abstract realm of politics and people's authentic and daily lives. **The repercussions extend beyond mere differences in opinion, manifesting intangible and often tragic outcomes that underline the importance of addressing the root causes of this divide.**

Corruption and Loss of Individual Freedoms We, as women, no longer have autonomy over our reproductive health. The purchase of at least two Supreme Court Justices and the influence of Donald Trump (so he claims) and other religious groups have impacted women in profound ways. Our lives are less than the fetus we carry. How can we be less than men as citizens? Is there legislation about a man's reproductive health? We know there is not.

CHAPTER 7

Bridging the Gap

Some initiatives and movements aim to foster dialog, understanding, and collaboration among people with different political views.

Better Angels (Now known as Braver Angels): This bipartisan network works to depolarize America by bringing liberals and conservatives together for workshops and debates to understand each other beyond stereotypes and form working alliances.

(https://braver angels.org/)

Bridge Alliance: A coalition of over ninety organizations working to provide support in a platform for a diverse array of efforts to revitalize democratic practice in America, emphasizing the importance of dialog and collaboration.

Living Room Conversations: An initiative encouraging people to host and participate in discussions about several topics, including politically charged issues, in a small, intimate setting to foster understanding and connection across differences.

All Sides: This platform provides news and issues from multiple points of view, aiming to break down filter bubbles and encourage readers to understand different perspectives.

The Village Square: A nonpartisan public educational forum that organizes programs and events to unite the community across political and ideological divides, focusing on civil dialog and debate.

Joint Ground Committee: Nonpartisan, nonprofit organization encouraging dialog and understanding among people with differing views through public forms and media content.

National Coalition for Dialogues and Deliberation (NCDD): An association of professionals and volunteers dedicated to solving social problems through organized dialog and deliberation efforts.

The Listen First Project: Through promoting the Listen First movement and the National Conversation project, this initiative has successfully engaged many partners and individuals in the mission to prioritize understanding and conversations. Success can be seen in the growing number of conversations facilitated, the diversity of participating organizations, and the widespread endorsement of the listened-first principles.

American Public Square: With its events featuring civil discourse on controversial subjects, it has successfully created spaces for constructive dialog. The presence of fact-checkers and a commitment to civility contribute to the organization's success in fostering informed and respectful discussions.

Convergence Center for Policy Resolution: convergence has brought stakeholders from various sectors together to solve policy issues. Its projects often result in actionable recommendations and have sometimes influenced policymaking and legislative efforts.

The impact of these initiatives is also evident in the personal testimonies of participants who report shifts in their perspectives, increased willingness to engage with opposing views, and a deeper understanding of complex issues.

Education is crucial in healing political divisions by fostering critical thinking, promoting media literacy, encouraging civic engagement, and cultivating student empathy and understanding.

Developing Critical Thinking Skills: Education helps individuals develop necessary thinking skills, enabling them to analyze arguments, identify biases, and consider multiple perspectives. This is essential for making informed decisions in a democratic society.

Promoting Media Literacy: Media literacy is vital in an era of information overload and widespread misinformation. Educational programs that teach students to evaluate sources critically, understand media bias, and discern credible information can reduce susceptibility to polarizing misinformation and propaganda.

Encouraging Civil Engagement: This program includes civic education components that can encourage students to participate actively in their communities and the democratic process. Understanding how government works, the importance of voting, and the value of participating in civic activities can empower individuals to contribute positively to society.

Cultivating Empathy and Understanding: Through exposure to diverse perspectives and histories, education can promote empathy and understanding. Courses that include multicultural education, social justice issues, and exploring diverse cultural and political backgrounds can help students appreciate the complexity of societal problems and the value of diverse viewpoints.

Teaching Conflict Resolution Skills: Incorporating conflict resolution and dialog skills into the curriculum can equip students with the tools to engage in constructive discussions, even when disagreements arise. Learning to listen, ask open-ended questions, and find common ground can be invaluable in personal and professional contexts and civic life.

Fostering a Culture of Respect and Inclusion: Educational environments that prioritize respect, inclusion, and democratic values can model the type of civil discourse necessary for a healthy democracy. Schools and colleges can serve as microcosms of society where students learn to engage respectfully and productively with people who have different opinions.

Preparing Informed Citizens: A well-rounded education prepares individuals to be informed citizens who can engage in meaningful debates, understand policy implications, and contribute to the democratic process in a knowledgeable manner. An emphasis on history, economics, political science, and environmental education can provide the context to understand current events and their broader implications.

Encouraging Lifelong Learning: Instilling a love for lifelong learning can help individuals remain open to current information and perspectives. This ongoing education can prevent the entrenchment of polarized views and promote a more dynamic and adaptable understanding of political and societal issues.

By addressing these aspects, education can play a pivotal role in healing political divisions and fostering a more informed, engaged, and empathetic citizenry capable of navigating the complexities of modern democratic life.

CHAPTER 8

Looking Ahead

The younger generation's demographic shifts will play a noteworthy role in shaping the future of American political discourse, potentially influencing it in several ways.

Diverse Perspectives and Values: younger generations, including Millennials and Gen X, have been shown to hold different values and attitudes on various issues compared to older generations, from climate change and social justice to technology and globalization.

They have more progressive stances on environmental sustainability, racial equality, LGBTQ + rights, and immigration and are likely to influence the topics and tone of political discourse.

Digital Natives and social media: As digital natives, younger generations are adept at social media and other digital platforms for organizing, activism, and sharing information.

This proficiency can amplify their political voices and expose them to challenging misinformation, echo chambers, and online polarization. Their engagement with these platforms will continue to shape these forces and reach political communication.

Increased Civic Engagement and Activism: There has been a notable increase in civic engagement and political activism among younger people, as seen in movements such as the March for Our Lives, the global climate strikes inspired by activists like Greta Thunberg, and the Black Lives Matter protest. This trend suggests that younger generations are willing to mobilize around critical issues, potentially leading to more grassroots involvement in demand for change in political discourse.

Changing Demographics: The United States is experiencing significant demographic chefs, increasing diversity in race, ethnicity, and cultural background. Younger generations are the most diverse in the United States history, influencing political priorities, policy debates, and the inclusivity of political discourse.

Impact on electoral politics: Younger voters are compromising an increasingly substantial portion of the electorate. Their preferences and turnout rates can significantly impact election outcomes, policy decisions, and political narratives. Politicians and parties may need to adapt their platforms and communication strategies to resonate with younger voters' concerns and communication styles.

Rejection of Polarization: Frustrated with the current level of polarization, including the current gridlock, younger generations may seek to change the tone and substance of political discourse, emphasizing consensus building, bipartisanship, and pragmatic solutions to complex problems.

Economic Priorities: Younger generations face unique financial challenges, job uncertainties, security and safety challenges, student loan debt, job market uncertainties, and worries about Social Security's future. These issues may become more central in political discourse, influencing debates on economic policy, educational reform, and social safety nets.

The involvement in the influence of younger generations and the impact of demographic shifts suggest a potentially transformative American political discourse with the potential for more inclusive, dynamic, and solution-oriented public dialog.

The political division in the United States faces several challenges that could intensify in the coming years. These challenges stem from societal, technological, economic, and political factors.

Increased Polarization: The trend of growing polarization, which caused the ideological gap between conservatives and liberals to widen, poses a significant challenge. This can lead to more extreme political positions, reduced willingness to compromise, and heightened animosity between opposing political groups.

Social Media and Misinformation Echo Chambers: All social media shapes political opinions and forms echo chambers. Individuals are exposed primarily to viewpoints reinforcing their beliefs, which can exacerbate divisions. The spread of misinformation and disinformation on these

Platforms further complicate the political landscape.

Economic Inequity: Rising economic inequality and the perception of an unfair financial system can fuel political discontent and division. Issues such as wage stagnation, job insecurity, and the wealth gap may drive wedges between different socioeconomic groups.

Demographic Shifts: the United States is experiencing significant demographic changes, including aging populations, increased racial and ethnic diversity, and changing immigration patterns. These can lead to cultural and generational misunderstandings and conflicts, influencing political allegiances and debates.

Technological Advancements and AI: Emerging technologies and artificial intelligence contribute to political division by enabling more sophisticated targeting of voters with polarizing content, deep fakes, and other forms of manipulated media that can undermine public discourse and trust. AI is already creating fake political ads for the upcoming elections. I have seen many fakes on more than one late-night comedy show.

Global Influences: International events and foreign interference in domestic politics can exaggerate divisions. Geopolitical conflicts, global economic shifts, and international campaigns to influence US politics through cyber operations or disinformation can deepen domestic divisions. Russia has been implicated in election attacks since 2016 on behalf of the Republican party.

Climate Change: Is the impact of climate change becoming more pronounced? Disagreements over environmental policies and the allocation of resources for mitigation and adaptation efforts could become more contentious, adding another layer to political debates.

The More In Common Foundation found that about 75% of Americans support gun laws and a path to citizenship, as we believe we have more in common. Our differences are not so great that we cannot find common ground.

We need to focus on the problem, the nuts and bolts of the problem, not the political affiliation. We need to have contact with different groups and explore their different perspectives.

We need town meetings where civil discourse is permitted, not rallies.

Citizens' Assemblies and meetings that could deliberate on challenging issues must include a genuine exchange of ideas.

The revolutionary technology in communication in our lifetimes may have promoted people to take sides.

Social Media companies encourage taking sides rather than taking perspectives. We need a more significant and unified sense of this nation to bridge our differences.

We could reframe the issues by tapping into the salient and striking commonalities of the problem, not the people or political affiliations.

Research indicates that people use partisan cues when evaluating policies.

Use referendums if a clear majority is reached; it could provide the beginning of a new social norm.

Engage in civil, respectful conversations with all people. We are all part of this world.

National voting standards and registration would improve this election across the nation.

Some successful examples of bipartisanship efforts include the CARES Act, a bipartisan response to COVID-19 passed in 2020.

The First Step Act, enacted in 2018, is a criminal justice reform bill to reduce recidivism and improve conditions in federal prisons.

The 21st Century Cures Act, signed in 2016, is focused on accelerating medical advances.

The Infrastructure Investment and Jobs Act was passed in 2021 to repair bridges and roads and provide broadband access. : replacing No Child Left Behind

Every Student Succeeds Act, replacing the No Child Left Behind Act, gives states more flexibility in education standards and accountability. (2015)

At least two bills have been stalled in the U.S. Senate since 2020. The For The People Act to reduce gerrymandering creates national standards for voter registration. Allow felons to vote after finishing their sentences and strengthen financial disclosure requirements.

The John Lewis Voter Rights Advancement Act

This would restore federal oversight of changes to election laws that could reduce the participation of voters, primarily when those changes disproportionately affect minority groups. However, national standards for Federal Elections may stabilize voter registration and access.

We need concerted efforts from everybody: political leaders, civil society, and individuals to foster dialog, compromise, and a shared commitment to democratic principles. Strategies might include electoral and institutional reforms, educational initiatives to improve media literacy and critical thinking, and rebuilding trust in democratic institutions.

Please do not surrender your vote.

References

Pew Research Center, November 9, 2021." Beyond Red vs Blue: The Political Topography"

Pew Research Center, November 22, 2021," Both Republicans and Democrats Prioritize family, but they differ over other sources of Meaning in Life."

Pew Research Center, January 25, 2022, "Biden Starts Year Two with Diminished Public Support and a Daunting List of Challenges."

https://www.newyorker.com/magazine/2021/03/15. "How Parties Die."

https: www.en.wikipedia.org/wiki. "Republican Party" _ (United States)."

https://www.usnews.com/topics/ subjects/republican-party.

(https:/braver anges.org./)

"Healing the Political Divide," Waldorff, Kirk, American Psychological Association, Vol.52, No.1, January 1, 2021.

September 10, 2020, French, David, "America is Being Pulled Apart. Here's How We Can Start to Heal Our Nation," Time Magazine.

De-Witt, Lee., Vân Der Linden, S., Brick, C, July 2, 2019., "What Are the Solutions to Political Polarization?"

April 27, 2021., Robinson, Gerald., "The Search for Unity: 4 ways Americans can bridge our racial and political divisions." USA Today.

National Institute for Civil Discourse (https://nicd.arizona.edu/)

www.ingramcontent.com/pod-product-compliance
Lightning Source LLC
Chambersburg PA
CBHW032103020426
42335CB00011B/471